LOOK FOR LISA

WHERE ARE THEY?

By
Anthony Tallarico

FANTAIL

FANTAIL PUBLISHING, AN IMPRINT OF PUFFIN ENTERPRISES
First published by Fantail Publishing, 1989
Penguin Books Canada Ltd.
10 Alcorn Avenue, Suite 300
Toronto, Ontario
M4V 3B2 Canada
Copyright © Kidsbooks Incorporated, 1989
All rights reserved
0140901469
Printed in the United States

LOOK FOR LISA AT THE MARATHON AND . . .

- ☑ Alien
- ☐ Alligator
- ☐ Ape
- ☐ Astronaut
- ☐ 2 Banana peels
- ☐ Barbell
- ☐ 5 Bats
- ☐ Big nose
- ☐ Cable car
- ☑ Cake
- ☑ Caveman
- ☐ 8 Chimneys
- ☐ Clown
- ☐ Convict
- ☐ Deep sea diver
- ☐ Drummer
- ☐ 2 Elephants
- ☐ Fire fighter
- ☐ Fish
- ☐ Flying carpet
- ☐ Football player
- ☐ Frankenstein monster
- ☐ Horse
- ☐ Ice skater
- ☐ Long-haired lady
- ☐ Man in a barrel
- ☐ Moose head
- ☐ Octopus
- ☐ Pig
- ☐ 6 Quitters
- ☐ Santa Claus
- ☐ Skier
- ☐ Sleeping jogger
- ☐ Snow White
- ☐ Tuba
- ☐ 2 Turtles
- ☐ Vampire
- ☐ Viking
- ☐ Waiter
- ☐ Worm

LOOK FOR LISA AFTER SCHOOL AND . . .

- ☐ Aeroplane
- ☐ 2 Aliens
- ☐ Beard
- ☐ Blackboard
- ☐ Books on wheels
- ☐ Bucket
- ☐ Bus driver
- ☐ "Class brain"
- ☐ Clown
- ☐ Coach
- ☐ Dog
- ☐ Fire hydrant
- ☐ Football player
- ☐ Ghost
- ☐ Hockey player
- ☐ "Junior"
- ☐ Litter bin
- ☐ Man trapped in a book
- ☐ 3 Mice
- ☐ Monkey
- ☐ Periscope
- ☐ Photographer
- ☐ Piano player
- ☐ Pillow
- ☐ "P.U."
- ☐ Pumpkin
- ☐ Rabbit
- ☐ Radio
- ☐ Sailor
- ☐ School mascot
- ☐ Scooter
- ☐ Shopping trolley
- ☐ Skateboard
- ☐ Ski jumper
- ☐ Socks
- ☐ Sports car
- ☐ Sunglasses
- ☐ Swing
- ☐ Tepee
- ☐ Top hat
- ☐ Unicorn

LOOK FOR LISA
AT THE ROCK
CONCERT AND . . .

- [ ] Alligator
- [ ] Apple
- [ ] Artist
- [ ] Beans
- [ ] Clown
- [ ] 2 Dogs
- [ ] Dwarf
- [ ] "Empty TV"
- [ ] Farmer
- [ ] Football
  player
- [ ] 4 Ghosts
- [ ] Giraffe
- [ ] 3 Guitars
- [ ] Heart
- [ ] 2 Hippos
- [ ] Hot dogs
- [ ] Hot foot
- [ ] Jogger
- [ ] Lamp post
- [ ] Lost balloon
- [ ] Magician
- [ ] "No Bus Stop"
- [ ] Pig
- [ ] Pink flamingo
- [ ] Pizza delivery
- [ ] Real cross
  wind
- [ ] Record albums
- [ ] 2 Robots
- [ ] Rock
- [ ] Rock queen
- [ ] Roll
- [ ] Rooster
- [ ] Scarecrow
- [ ] School bus
- [ ] Skateboard
- [ ] 15 Speakers
- [ ] Stars
- [ ] Tent
- [ ] "Too Heavy
  Metal"
- [ ] Turtle
- [ ] Witch
- [ ] Zebra

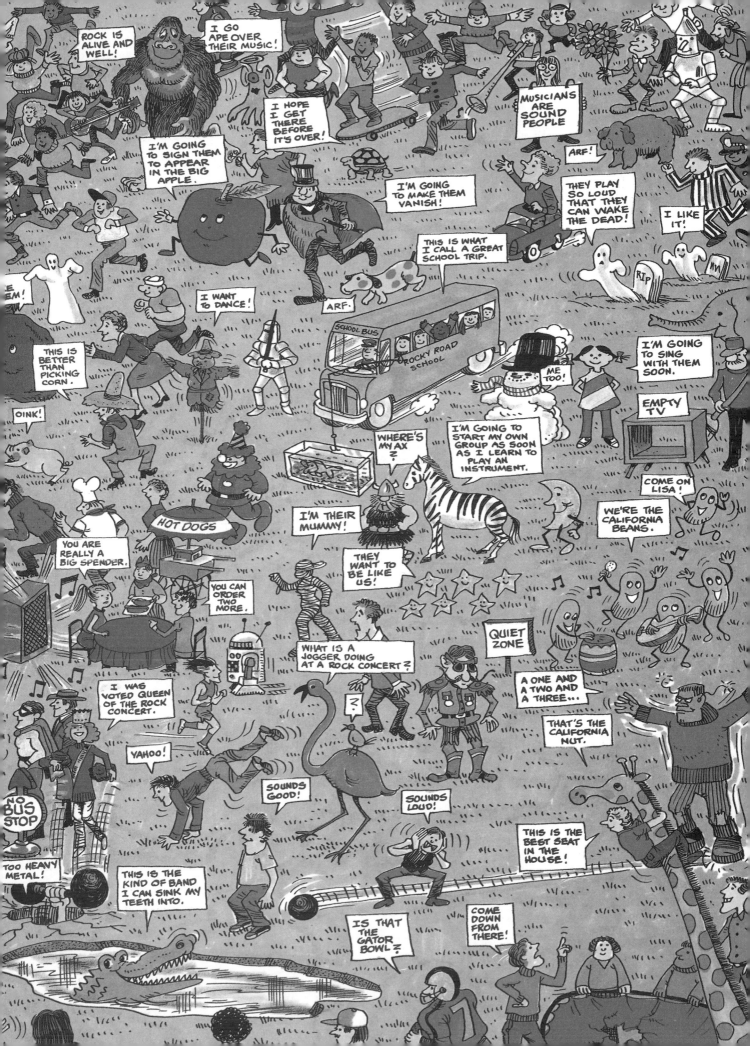

LOOK FOR LISA ON THE FARM AND . . .

LOOK FOR LISA AT THE BEACH AND . . .

- ☐ Artist
- ☐ Barrel of pickles
- ☐ Birdbath
- ☐ Boot
- ☐ 3 Bottles with notes
- ☐ Bubblegum
- ☐ 4 Cactuses
- ☐ 2 Clowns
- ☐ Cow
- ☐ Crocodile
- ☐ Dart thrower
- ☐ 4 Flying fish
- ☐ Hammerhead shark
- ☐ Leaking boat
- ☐ Life belt
- ☐ Litterbug
- ☐ Lost bathing suit
- ☐ 3 Mermaids
- ☐ Motorcyclist
- ☐ Mummy
- ☐ Musician
- ☐ Oil rig
- ☐ Pirate ship
- ☐ Polluted area
- ☐ 3 Radios
- ☐ Robinson Crusoe
- ☐ Rowboat
- ☐ Sailfish
- ☐ Seahorse
- ☐ Sea serpent
- ☐ Sleeping man
- ☐ Skull cave
- ☐ Stingray
- ☐ Submarine
- ☐ 6 Surfboards
- ☐ Telescope
- ☐ Thief
- ☐ Tricyclist
- ☐ Very quick sand
- ☐ 2 Water skiers

LOOK FOR LISA AROUND THE WORLD AND . . .

- ☐ Bear
- ☐ Big foot
- ☐ 2 Bridge builders
- ☐ Cactus
- ☐ Camel
- ☐ Cowboy
- ☐ Cup of coffee
- ☐ Cup of tea
- ☐ Dog
- ☐ Eskimo
- ☐ 12 Fish
- ☐ 2 Flying saucers
- ☐ Golfer
- ☐ Heart
- ☐ Ice castle
- ☐ Igloo
- ☐ Kangaroo
- ☐ Lighthouse
- ☐ Lion
- ☐ Mermaid
- ☐ Merman
- ☐ Oil well
- ☐ Ox
- ☐ 6 Penguins
- ☐ Rock singer
- ☐ 4 Sailboats
- ☐ Sea serpent
- ☐ 4 Skiers
- ☐ 2 Snowmen
- ☐ Stuck ship
- ☐ Submarine
- ☐ 3 Surfers
- ☐ Telescope
- ☐ 6 "Travel Agent" signs
- ☐ Tug boat
- ☐ T.V. set
- ☐ Unicorns in Utah
- ☐ Viking ship
- ☐ Walrus
- ☐ Whale

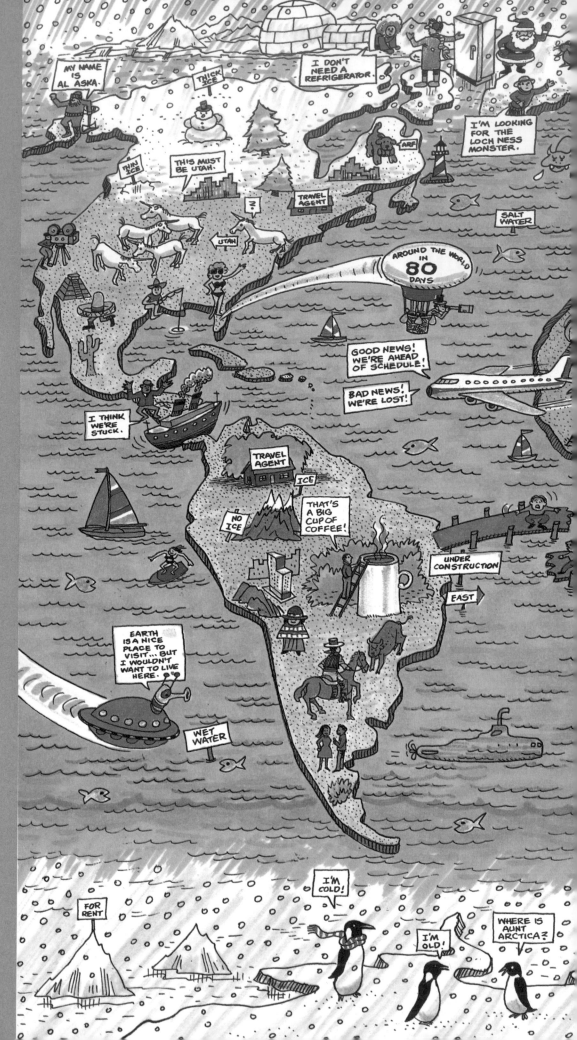

LOOK FOR LISA AT THE LIBRARY AND . . .

- ☐ Angel
- ☐ Banana peel
- ☐ Baseball cap
- ☐ Basketball players
- ☐ Book in a bottle
- ☐ 2 Bowling balls
- ☐ 4 Bullet holes
- ☐ Caveman
- ☐ Clown
- ☐ 2 Cowboys
- ☐ Doctor
- ☐ Flying saucer
- ☐ Football
- ☐ Giant
- ☐ Hamburger
- ☐ Hammer
- ☐ Happy face
- ☐ 4 Hearts
- ☐ Hockey stick
- ☐ Horse
- ☐ Hula hoop
- ☐ Humpty Dumpty
- ☐ Moon
- ☐ Mummy and child
- ☐ Palm tree
- ☐ Paper plane
- ☐ 2 Parrots
- ☐ Photocopier
- ☐ Pizza
- ☐ 7 "Quiet" signs
- ☐ 2 Radios
- ☐ Red trolley
- ☐ Referee
- ☐ Ship
- ☐ Skis
- ☐ 3 Skulls
- ☐ Telescope
- ☐ Tennis racket
- ☐ Tiny people
- ☐ TV camera
- ☐ Vacuum cleaner
- ☐ Worn tyre

LOOK FOR LISA
AT THE
AMUSEMENT PARK
AND . . .

- ☐ Astronaut
- ☐ 15 Balloons
- ☐ Baseball
- ☐ Bomb
- ☐ Cactus
- ☐ Cheese
- ☐ Diplodocus
- ☐ "Do Not Read This"
- ☐ Entrance
- ☐ Exit
- ☐ Fishing hole
- ☐ 5 Ghosts
- ☐ Gorilla
- ☐ Headless man
- ☐ High diver
- ☐ Horse
- ☐ "Hot Dogs"
- ☐ "House of Horrors"
- ☐ "Kisses"
- ☐ Litter bin
- ☐ "Low Tide"
- ☐ 4 Mice
- ☐ 3 Monsters
- ☐ Mummy
- ☐ "No U-Turns"
- ☐ Pear
- ☐ Rocket
- ☐ Santa Claus
- ☐ Schoolmaster
- ☐ "Scrambled Eggs"
- ☐ Skateboard
- ☐ Skull
- ☐ Snowman
- ☐ Thirteen o'clock
- ☐ Umbrella
- ☐ Vampire
- ☐ Witch

LOOK FOR LISA AT THE FLEA MARKET AND . . .

LOOK FOR LISA AS THE CIRCUS COMES TO TOWN AND . . .

LOOK FOR LISA

FIND FREDDIE

SEARCH FOR SAM

HUNT FOR HECTOR